BIG PICTURE 📷 SPORTS

Meet the
NEW ENGLAND
PATRIOTS

BY
ZACK BURGESS

NORWOODHOUSE PRESS

CHICAGO, ILLINOIS

NORWOOD HOUSE PRESS

P.O. Box 316598 • Chicago, Illinois 60631
For more information about Norwood House Press please visit our website at
www.norwoodhousepress.com or call 866-565-2900.

Photo Credits:
All photos courtesy of Associated Press, except for the following: Black Book Archives (6, 7, 15, 18, 22),
Topps, Inc. (10 both, 11 all), Sports Illustrated for Kids (23).

Cover Photo: Gregory Payan/Associated Press

The football memorabilia photographed for this book is part of the authors' collection. The collectibles used
for artistic background purposes in this series were manufactured by many different card companies—
including Bowman, Donruss, Fleer, Leaf, O-Pee-Chee, Pacific, Panini America, Philadelphia Chewing Gum,
Pinnacle, Pro Line, Pro Set, Score, Topps, and Upper Deck—as well as several food brands, including
Crane's, Hostess, Kellogg's, McDonald's and Post.

Designer: Ron Jaffe
Series Editors: Mike Kennedy and Mark Stewart
Project Management: Black Book Partners, LLC.
Editorial Production: Lisa Walsh

LIBRARY OF CONGRESS CATALOGING-IN-PUBLICATION DATA
Names: Burgess, Zack.
Title: Meet the New England Patriots / by Zack Burgess.
Description: Chicago, Illinois : Norwood House Press, [2016] | Series: Big
  picture sports | Includes bibliographical references and index. |
  Audience: Grade: K to Grade 3.
Identifiers: LCCN 2015026329| ISBN 9781599537429 (Library Edition : alk.
  paper) | ISBN 9781603578455 (eBook)
Subjects: LCSH: New England Patriots (Football team)--Miscellanea--Juvenile
  literature.
Classification: LCC GV956.N36 B87 2016 | DDC 796.332/640974461--dc23
LC record available at http://lccn.loc.gov/2015026329

288N—072016
Manufactured in the United States of America in North Mankato, Minnesota

CONTENTS

Words in **bold type** are defined on page 24.

The Patriots have great team spirit.

4

CALL ME A PATRIOT

Patriots defend their country at all costs. That was the attitude of the men and women who began the fight for freedom that created the United States. The New England Patriots honor those heroes every time they take the field. No team works harder to win.

TIME MACHINE

The Patriots played their first season in 1960. They were part of the **American Football League (AFL)**. In 1970, the "Pats" joined the National Football League (NFL). They have always relied on great leaders. Tom Brady and **Richard Seymour** were two of the best.

Tom Brady scans the field for an open receiver.

There is never an empty seat at a Patriots game.

Best Seat in the House

New England includes the states of Massachusetts, Connecticut, Vermont, Maine, and New Hampshire. The Patriots' stadium has features that remind fans of this region. The most famous is a lighthouse that stands in the open end of the field.

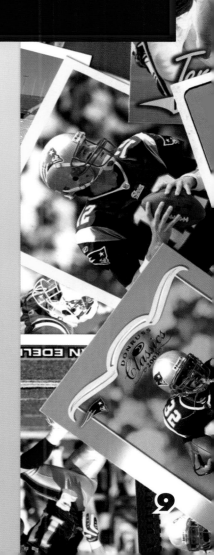

SHOE BOX

The trading cards on these pages show some of the best Patriots ever.

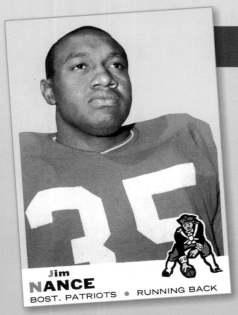

JIM NANCE

RUNNING BACK • 1965–1971

Jim was the AFL's most powerful runner. He was named the league's top player in 1966.

SAM CUNNINGHAM

RUNNING BACK • 1973–1982

Sam was impossible to stop when the Patriots were near the end zone. His nickname was "Sam the Bam."

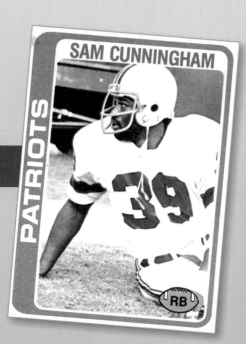

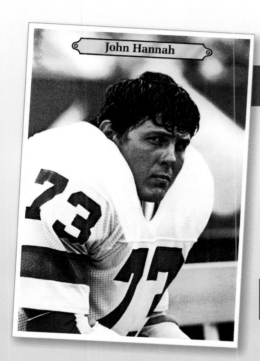

John Hannah

JOHN HANNAH

GUARD · 1973-1985

John used great speed and strength to block opponents. He was an **All-Pro** seven times.

ADAM VINATIERI

KICKER · 1996-2005

Adam loved to kick field goals with the game on the line. He helped the Patriots win three Super Bowls.

ADAM VINATIERI
KICKER   NEW ENGLAND PATRIOTS

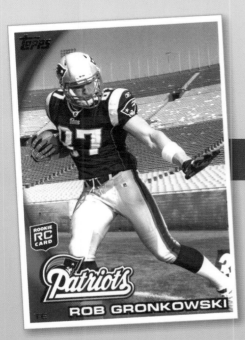

ROB GRONKOWSKI

ROB GRONKOWSKI

TIGHT END · FIRST YEAR WITH TEAM: 2010

"Gronk" was a nightmare to cover. He set an NFL record for tight ends with 17 touchdowns in 2011.

The Big Picture

Look at the two photos on page 13. Both appear to be the same. But they are not. There are three differences. Can you spot them?

Answers on page 23.

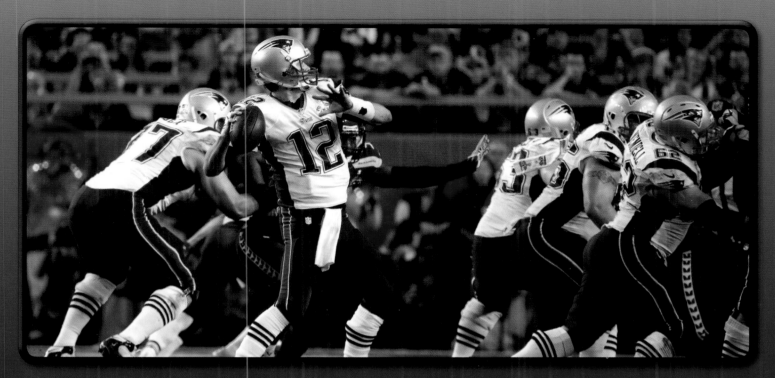

TRUE OR FALSE?

Tom Brady was a star quarterback. Two of these facts about him are **TRUE**. One is **FALSE**. Do you know which is which?

1 Tom once threw 162 passes in a row without an **interception**.

2 Tom is the great-great grandson of George Washington.

3 Tom was the Most Valuable Player in the Super Bowl three times.

Answer on page 23.

Winning the Super Bowl was always on Tom Brady's mind.

New England fans reach for a souvenir.

Go Patriots, Go!

Patriots fans love their team with all their heart. The players show the same support in return. People who root for the Patriots often see their favorite stars in public. They think of them as their neighbors. The Patriots feel the same way.

ON THE MAP

Here is a look at where five Patriots were born, along with a fun fact about each.

1 **TEDY BRUSCHI · SAN FRANCISCO, CALIFORNIA**
Tedy led the team's defense in three Super Bowl wins.

2 **WES WELKER · OKLAHOMA CITY, OKLAHOMA**
Wes was the NFL's leading receiver three times with the Patriots.

3 **GINO CAPPELLETTI · KEEWATIN, MINNESOTA**
Gino was the team's best receiver in the 1960s.

4 **ANDRE TIPPETT · BIRMINGHAM, ALABAMA**
Andre had 100 **quarterback sacks** for the Patriots.

5 **SEBASTIAN VOLLMER · DUSSELDORF, GERMANY**
Sebastian used the footwork he learned in soccer to become a great blocker.

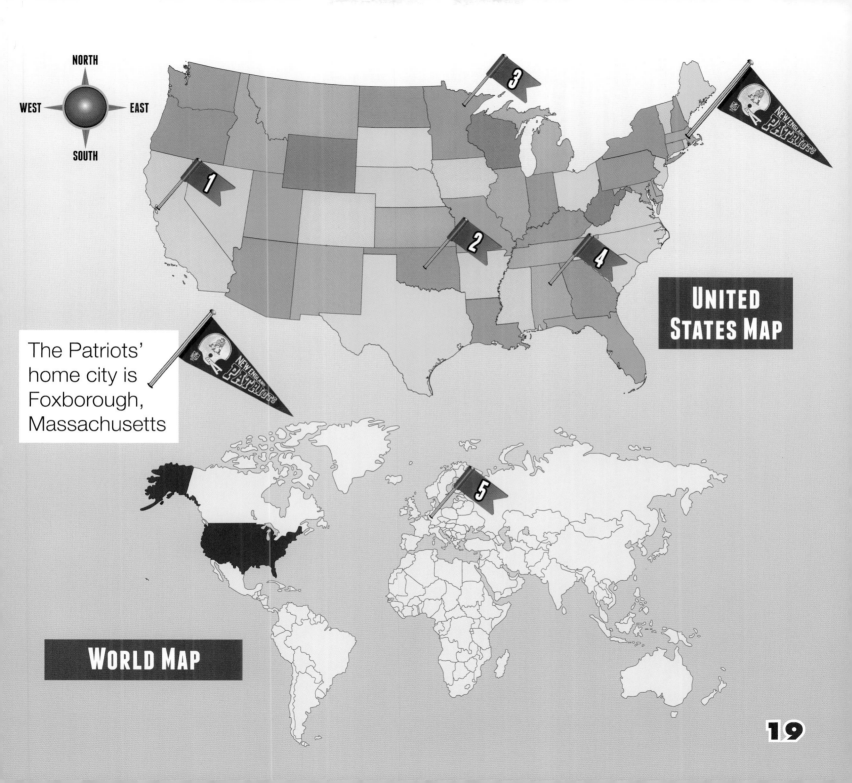

NORTH

WEST ● EAST

SOUTH

The Patriots' home city is Foxborough, Massachusetts

UNITED STATES MAP

WORLD MAP

Julian Edelman wears the Patriots' home uniform.

Football teams wear different uniforms for home and away games. The main colors of the Patriots have always been red, white, and blue. In 1993, the team began using silver, too.

20

The Patriots' helmet is silver. There is a cartoon of a patriot on each side. Fans like to call him "Pat the Patriot."

Rob Gronkowski wears the Patriots' away uniform.

WE WON!

The Patriots reached the Super Bowl for the first time at the end of the 1985 season. They won their first NFL championship 16 years later. They repeated as champions three times in the next 14 years. **Bill Belichick** was the coach for all four titles.

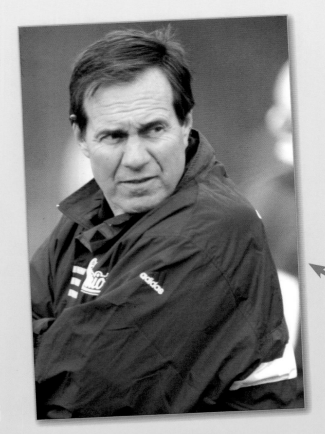

RECORD BOOK

These Patriots set team records.

TOUCHDOWN PASSES	RECORD
Season: Tom Brady (2007)	50
Career: Tom Brady	428

TOUCHDOWN CATCHES	RECORD
Season: Randy Moss (2007)	23
Career: Stanley Morgan	67

RUSHING TOUCHDOWNS	RECORD
Season: **Curtis Martin** (1995 & 1996)	14
Career: Jim Nance	45

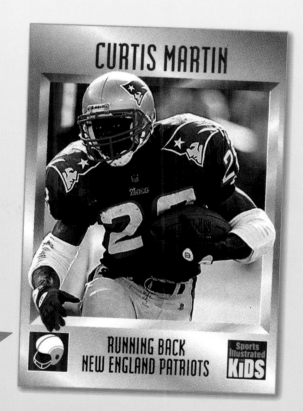

CURTIS MARTIN

RUNNING BACK
NEW ENGLAND PATRIOTS

Sports Illustrated KIDS

ANSWERS FOR THE BIG PICTURE
The 7 in #77 changed to 9, the logo on #12's helmet changed, and #12's towel disappeared.

ANSWER FOR TRUE AND FALSE
#2 is false. Tom is not the great-great grandson of George Washington.

Football Words

All-Pro
An honor given to the best NFL player at each position.

American Football League (AFL)
A rival league of the NFL that played from 1960 to 1969.

Interception
A pass caught by a defensive player.

Quarterback Sacks
Tackles of the quarterback that lose yardage.

Index

Photos are on **BOLD** numbered pages.

ABOUT THE AUTHOR

Zack Burgess has been writing about sports for more than 20 years. He has lived all over the country and interviewed lots of All-Pro football players, including Brett Favre, Eddie George, Jerome Bettis, Shannon Sharpe, and Rich Gannon. Zack was the first African American beat writer to cover Major League Baseball when he worked for the *Kansas City Star*.

ABOUT THE PATRIOTS

Learn more at these websites:

www.patriots.com • www.profootballhof.com

www.teamspiritextras.com/Overtime/html/patriots.html